I0190715

Poems
of
Life

Books by the Anonymous Author and Artist

Life's Heart Break: A Novella

In the end, will Zenald discover what may be one of life's biggest heart-breaks: heart-ache?

Duty & Destruction I

A real female experiences life in and out of the U.S. military.

Life's Poetic Dichotomies

Some of life's biggest dichotomies are juxtaposed poetically.

Her Poetic Rise

It is for the religiously poetic that blends religion and feminism.

Life's Short Stories

Fictional characters vie to live their own lives.

Life's Mixed Poetry

Poems are mixed schematically, stylistically, and randomly.

Life's Novellas: Fate Waits Upon No One

The good and the bad are juxtaposed, chronologically, fictionally, and theatrically.

Their Poetic Minds

Poems are juxtaposed, religiously, femininely, and dichotomously.

Art Book

The Diamond & Heart Art Collections

Pictures are exhibited, categorically, by coloring schemes and coloring mediums; all of which, have been affected with special effects.

Schemes: pastel shades; earth tones; primary colors; gray, black and white; black and white.

Mediums: colored pencils; water coloring; pastel coloring; acrylic coloring; oil coloring.

Poems
of
Life

Anonymous

Century Conquests

Poems of Life

Copyright © 2013 by Anonymous

All rights reserved. Printed in the United States of America. No part of this book may be used or reproduced in any way, at all, without written permission from the publisher, except, in the case of brief quotations embodied in critical articles or reviews.

www.centuryconquests.com
info@centuryconquests.com

ISBN: 978-0-9850698-7-2

Cover graphic designed by: Century Conquests © 2013

Century Conquests ® 2012

Poems
of
Life

Anonymous

Acknowledgements

Once more, for the small voice deep inside me that wants me to carry on poetically.

I thank each person that has helped with the publication of this book.

I even thank each reader of my book for indulging my mixture of poetry and all that it involves.

Life has its poetry, whose poems are almost always mixed.

A.

Part 1

Whistle a Different Tune

…Transformation…!

…Transformable….

…Transform….

…Transforming….

…Transformative….

…Transformer….

…Transforms….

…Transformed….

I'm now a totally transformative transformer having since transformed a transformable transform; whose transformation just wasn't transforming, fast, enough…!

Peace and Quiet

I almost certainly try to have lots of it, Peace;

Since, it's what almost always loves my company, a fabulous feast.

Photograph of the Man

The man is standing in the heart of the vastly golden-green-colored field.

Native trees are ample as are the native plants that are growing from its lush soil.

The man's small or slim yet solid body suggests his labor on the ranch.

His face is seeable—somewhat, under a broad sun hat.

Beneath it, his brownish-red-colored hair is just blowing in the freshly country air.

He's mindful of the fantastic fire-ball that is just dangling in the azure-colored sky.

Still, under that broadly big hat—it, I see some of his handsome face:

Its striking features; smooth complexion; vigorous glow….

His super sweet smile is even signifying how at ease he is with his rural life and all.

Doesn't his every-day and dis-colored denim, cover-alls—or, over-alls,

Even signify a pretty photogenic photo of this man's life?

"Tomorrow, I'll begin to transform my life," says the poetic character.

Character: Tomorrow, I'll begin to transform my life.
Me: Why tomorrow of all days…?

Character: Well, it'll be a good day to do so….
Me: Uh-huh.

Me: Truly, why've you chosen tomorrow, in particular, to transform your life?
Character: Well, today's my last day of bein' a super sure sinner.

Me: Oh?
Character: That's right! I'm about finished sinnin'.

Me: How'll you change?
Character: Hum, my faith is much stronger….

Me: What kind of faith…?
Character: Of course, Hinduism.

Me: Why Hinduism?
Character: Because, I like what it stands for, soundly, or roundly.

Me: What does it signifies or symbolizes?
Character: I'm interested mostly in the importance that it puts on meditation….

Me: Huh-uh. Do you've a supportable system…?
Character: Say what? Nope—I don't care for one because I've my *own* goddamn power…!

Me: Oh? You're doing it all, alone?
Character: I sure am!

Me: Tell me, please, what's the *new you* looking to get in return for this self-styled change…?
Character: Well, I'd like to see all of my delicious dreams come true and my nasty nightmares stay away or just remain at bay…!

Nature's Day

Thunder roaring
Stars glimmering
Fluffy clouds flying
One quarter of a moon standing guard
In a blackish-gray sky
All a part of nature's day.

Lightning crackling
Stars glowing
Clouds vanishing
One-half of a moon standing guard
In a grayish-black sky
All a part of nature's day.

Raindrops falling
Stars shining
Cotton-candy clouds floating
Three quarters of a moon standing guard
In a blackish-blue sky
All a part of nature's day.

Ice crystals dropping
Stars beaming
Clouds passing
Full moon standing guard
In a bluish-black sky
All a part of nature's day.

Up-Roar

Never mind, that, that fabulous feast of a beast causes me to Fuss;

I still must obey it, even though its gluttonous appetite often makes me cuss!

A Super Seller
(A Found Poem)

Miami Beach Condos

The Miami Beach Condo Specialist

Zerk Zenith: Licensed Real Estate Broker/Agent

1000 Alton Road, Suite # 0001

Miami Beach, Florida 33140

305.098.7654

www.ZerkZenith.com

Zerk@Hotmail.com

Ten-Strike

The hard-working female almost certainly garners her Success.

Neither is it just some pretty prized hour.

That she prettily, and boldly, or heroically out-wits life's hardest tests.

Don't be wrong, either, by questioning her *super staying power*.

Because the female seeks to always out-best.

Nor would anything ev'r mess up her success—un-less,

She stops wanting to be the very best: or, out-do all of life's terribly thorny tests.

State of Affairs

Really, whose is it, Life?

And, why does hers have such strife?

Is it because of him: or, her husband's jaggedly dark knife?

It's true, too, that the two almost always fight;

That's right, for the couple almost nev'r misses a damn single bite.

Also, they just love biting off of each other at night.

Since, the darkly bright-color'd couple are all about slight.

Or, they're quite full of malicious-making might!

That's right; the two almost nev'r dream, economically, about making things right;

For, they simply can't and won't bear the pretty painful price!

That is, he and she both want or need to be the one that endures life!

.

Part 2

Nightmares

Nightmares, nightmares…? Yes!

Nightmares aren't only for those who sleep;

But, they're ev'n for those who drift right into the blue-black deep.

Nightmares, nightmares…? Yes, nightmares!

The sub-conscious mind comes alive when the body dives deeply into deep sleep.

Traveling, traveling, and traveling right—along, into the up-most un-known:

A space or place where the every-day mind fails to record, roundly, the deep and dark or even nightmarish wants, and needs, or fears….

Nightmares or damnably dark dreams converse for the un-conscious—or,

The sub-conscious mind….

Nightmares…? Nightmares! Yes, nightmares.

Deep and dark and even nasty or even nastily dark or even darkly deep nightmares….

Nightmares—oh yes—nightmares…!

Physical Condition

Something is just as important as his increasable Health:

His soul's imminent death;

This is why, exactly, he ought not to clinch closely his damnably hard-earned wealth.

Not Make the Grade

The know-it-all, all-powerful, big-headed, and self-important, and ev'n cash-hungry female definitely detests any kind of let-down.

Yet, her super sour smugness almost certainly causes her to be a circular clown.

Just, the same, that she almost nev'r likes to Fall Short;

Or, that, you'll almost nev'r hear her gloat!

Such makes it quite possible for her to hit on or stumble upon some one;

Note, too, that he or she ought not to be about any sort of damn fun!

On the Go
Enjambment—Rest & Relaxation/Recuperation (R&R)

Come right to a halt and hush all noise

      Get right out of the motor car and get right to the front door.

Push right in the security code

        And get right inside.

Flop right down on the settee

          And lean right back—or, just, relax!

Ill Health

YEEEK! The shady, mucky, and dicey leech likes taking it to him, evilness.

That's correct, and the female leech almost certainly takes it at night time.

Since dimness almost certainly hides such Illness.

Vest In

To the shabby and silly mores of woman-kind, they'll almost nev'r yield.

HURRAH!

For the brawny and brainy mores of man-kind has almost always been sealed;

Given that, they aren't a stark-naked bunch of nuts.

To all those who would inquire about their guts;

Know that such inquisition will be immediately killed.

To like them or not, it's basically your pick;

Howev'r, consider, that the men have a super solid stance—that, almost, certainly, can't or won't ev'r be kicked.

AES RHTSILUTRE

(Some Super Surrealism)

His mind is a round roller coaster that's zoomin' roundly and right out of control
     whose thoughts are wintergreens and made of yellow gelatins
Whose ego is just as big as The Dark Continent
     whose motives appear and disappear
     when there's somethin' to be gain'd and somethin' to be lost
Whose body is an isosceles triangle
     whose points pierce his internal organs
     whose feel is just as gray jelly
Whose skin is the color of rust and as rough as the skin of an alien from the planet Pluto
Whose hair is a camp-fire
     whose smell is just as over-cook'd straw
Whose head is a pitcher that's empty on a half-full day
     whose sound is just as thunder
Whose brain is but a drop of water that turns to vapor and evaporates
     whose taste is just as beige chocolate
Whose ears hear micro-wave transmissions
     whose feel is just as tin-plate
Whose eyes see the woman in the moon, and a green cock-roach crawlin' right into
     heaven with hopes of findin' black devilish eggs
Whose nose is a double-canal for funneling polluted air
     whose shape is just as a big crooked pecan
Whose mouth is a barbeque pit
     whose tongue is charcoal-color'd
     whose voice crackles just as summer lightnin'
     whose texture is just as lamb fur
Whose hands are creatures from the deep purple sea
     whose fingers are lobster legs that's been chew'd by an orange barracuda
     whose finger-nails are fibrous proteins
     whose feel is just as satin
Whose legs are out-side calipers
     whose texture is just as barb'd wire
     whose feet are giant leaves
     whose toes are infect'd with an utterly un-holy fungus
     whose feel is just as wet bakin' soda
Whose heart is the shape of a super sour grape that's been crush'd by Big Foot
     whose color is blue-black
Whose old clothes is made of hard paper and wear just as 500-year-old outer skin

Whose values are pink earth-worms
      whose texture is just as a bizarre rain-bow
      on a damnably dark and a wickedly winter night that'll nev'r see the break of day
Whose character is all but naught
Whose love is just as sweet as pig feet and as bitter as blue vinegar
      whose feel is just as brown clay
Whose charm is just as small as a dot of dust
      whose color is just as white gold
      whose texture is just as leather
      whose smell is just as carbon
      whose taste is just as bitter-sweet as blood-color'd berries
Whose life just zig-zags on a plastic roller coaster through a cloudy tunnel under-ground
      whose existence is forsaken—and, fantastically, just, as a pregnant trans-sexual;
      yet, on a day of no shape or sound nor color nor texture nor smell nor taste;
      on a day that don't ev'n exist—but, in the mind of *The Surrealist.*

Dereliction of Duty

The utterly un-attractive and total time-waster of a female is almost certainly on edge.

Why's that?

Perhaps, it's because of her monstrously mis-guided mis-obligation that's just like a wedge.

In lieu of standing guard duty, she, almost, always, prefers, instead, to waste time, most wastefully, by guarding a super sweet potato pie.

This is why, precisely, that Uncle Sam intends to down grade; and, cast off; and even, turn his back on the woefully wasteful female—right, in the midst of her half-empty pledge.

That's right, for there's always a darn high cost of a toll.

Rightly, and merely, there'll be no more darn'd mold (or rot) on the watch.

Since, such will continue—only, to cause the soul-less, and list-less, or super sluggish slacker of a female, to fold right into a really round rut of an un-prettily plump roll.

HORRAY!

.

Part 3

Answer Up
(A Poem of Dialogue)

"You're un-stable. So, how can I depend on you?"

"I know that I'm sometimes un-steady."

"You're un-balanced and un-wise and I can't depend on you."

"I know that I'm sometimes ill-advised or mis-guided…."

"You're self-indulgent. So, tell me, how can I depend on you, ev'r?"

"I know that I'm sometimes self-absorbed and…."

"You're thought-less of yourself and ev'n me. I can't depend on you."

"I know that I'm sometimes care-less or un-mindful…."

"You're spirit-less and value-less. So, pretty please, tell me that I can't depend on you."

"I know that I'm sometimes no-good—or, of no-account."

"You're down-right un-dependable, and I can't or won't ev'r depend on you!"

"I know that you can't or won't ev'r depend on me, down-rightly."

Bomb-Shell

Sky black-blue; complex vacant;
     Insects sound asleep; community silent;
          The dwelling still appears welcoming.

Walk fast; beat hard;
     Eaves-drop cautiously; linger patiently;
          Someone just has to come to the door.

Stare shockingly; question civilly;
     Take note, fixedly; back slide, bit by bit;
          As that, someone emerges to my absolute astonishment.

Twirl around; I'm shame to state—
     That someone isn't supposed to be here—or, there;
          Yet, that someone—oh hell—well!

I just don't accept it, and I still can't accept it;
     That, I've to vanish into the blue-black night—
          Though, silently, I'm astonished….

Be Keen On

When one has it, how long does it stay—Love?

This is to ask—or, say: that, it'll ultimately go away like an adulterously

Adventurous dove.

Till I'm sure…, I'll bide time, only, in my pretty, lively, and downy

Bath tub….

It's where I often-times get a piece of love—instead of, at a parasitically masculine pub.

Steel-Heartedness

Please, or pretty please, just call me Cole.

      Howev'r, I must admit that such isn't my true name.

            Just, the same, that the name or Cole could or would nev'r be lame;

                  It's because I'm almost always Bold!

                        That I almost certainly hold on while on the damn'd go!

                Since, I can't—or, won't permit my truly good name, ev'r, to be in vain!

Just the same, that I'll forev'r stay a part of life's goddamn'd dog-eat-male—game!

To be bravely bold, it's also, almost, always, how I've to handle my damn dough!

.

The Space

It's an up-scale yet down-to-earth and pretty place of a space.

The super select suburb is enmeshed amidst a beauteous back-drop.

The amorous air is gusting—and, lively leaves are dropping from nearby trees.

The lights are giving the setting a rather golden glow or radiance.

The beautiful back-ground and gold-looking homes—all, are exhibiting an uppity-ness.

The neighborhood appears or seems to be upper-class.

The stylish yet straight-thinking people are even lingering about a great big pool.

Most are just lingering around, drinking, smoking, chatting, and cuddling, and even body-watching.

Some are experiencing the wildly warm whirl-pool.

Others are soaking up both saunas' mugginess—dry, and steamy.

Right, on cue, an utterly un-tannish woman jumps into the sapphire-colored pool.

She floats first and then starts to swim most suitably.

Her muscled arms are cutting right through the curvy water with such style and skill.

Her toughened legs or hard-edge kicks are some pretty powerful propellers.

Right now, the super sound of some soulfully slick song, foot-steps, and all, means, that the night's life is about to begin, in effect, and rather un-tastefully. HOOPLA!

A Bright Acquaintance

We're acquainted and then we communicated then we became more than just
acquaintances;

     Yet, I've felt as though I've always known you.

We became co-workers and then you became my boss;

     Yet, I've felt as though you could've or would've never asserted your rank.

We dined together and then we went to a joyously jazzy concert together.

     Yet, I've felt as though we've been together—almost, forever.

We needn't say good-by, either, to each other, ever.

     And, on this day, I can say—only, that you're a beautifully bright acquaintance;

       Who, obviously, trusts just as much as I trust in the potently pure power
of together-ness.

Heaviness of Heart

The woman's dream has been to nev'r experience any real Heart Break.

Still, life's full of utterly un-avoidable bolts, or better, utterly un-avoidable shocks.

Like an illegitimately un-loyal, un-lovable, and un-loved man;

Who's been, of course, taken right to the bank.

Thus, the thing that the man and the woman both should do—only, is to now turn,

roundly, right, into rectangular-styled rocks.

Big Baby

The male would nev'r be some sort of tooth-less Coward.
Not like some female or fantastic fraidy-cat that instead wants to snatch him back or weigh him down.

In other words, nothing could or would ev'r make him turn into a fearfully un-colorful clown.

Since, he intends to be the marvelously multi-colored man of the hour: It's the type of roundly reddish-yellow-colored power; which, almost, always, keeps the male's power super sound.

That's correct. For he'll nev'r be snatched back or weighed down—BAM!

Yet again, he's bound or wound to duty; whose very values of life and methods of living it, life, are colorfully circular or circularly colorful;

Un-like a down-rightly down-and-out clown's fantastically feeble frown.
He's once again wound—or, duty-bound; to some pretty powerful principles of life, and utterly unmatchable methodologies by which it ought to be liv'd: his damn'd life.

No frown's ev'r allowed—ev'n, when he's way down to the damn ground.
WHAM!

Fatal Outcome

What's similar to life's super sharpest knife?

Is it where one finishes up—after life?

Without doubt, that such inquiry shouldn't be a topic for static blather.

Why not? Well, it's because such subject-matter must be weathered.

That is, whether one finishes up in the after life or the here after or even in between is of

top-most importance.

For such will almost always embody one's total tolerance.

Or, better yet, would one much rather exist in life, enduring not some much higher

ideology of life and methodology by which it ought to be lived—life; but, instead,

enduring one's own self-inflicted, self-appointed, and self-centered provisions?

If so, then, pretty, please, keep in mind that one—and, no one else, will report as much:

Account for one's own ideas—or, nakedly nefarious visions.

Part 4

My Ev'r-Lasting Friend

I see you nowadays just as I've almost always seen you:
You're wonderful and polite and even kind—humorous.

I see you nowadays just as I've almost always seen you:
You're welcoming and compassionate and even forgiving—loving.

I see you nowadays just as I've almost always seen you:
You're supportive and hopeful and even faithful—generous.

I see you nowadays just as I've almost always seen you:
You're unquestionably my un-ending friend of a smart, strong,
    and successful; or, you're an honorably self-respectful female.

Utopia

The female comic experiences such Happiness.

Nor need she hoard—not, one single knife.

Since her marvelously multi-colored life, almost, always, tolerates no type of sadness.

That's so correct; for her circularly comical way of life has hardly any strife.

As such gladness, almost, certainly, contributes to her absolute aptness.

At Present
(A Sense Experience)

I'm just sitting here at a patio table on the patio.

And, lately, my pencil has become weighty, and, woefully.

Perhaps, my writing and all is way too wide-ranging.

My environment is all but mind numbing.

Earth's utterly usual creatures are monotonous in my sight.

The same old sounds … are even repetitive, and soundly, if not roundly.

I'm due, most definitely, for some brand new surroundings.

I'll let you know—why…, soon, enough.

Looking up, I'm seeing a cloudily azurean sky.

Un-seeable birds are conversing, circularly, and a few butterflies are flying around.

Then, unbelievably, I see the most beautiful of birds:

Its colorfully reddish-orange color is pretty portentous;

That, some things are coming right into focus, quite, frankly.

Still, I'm just so damn tired of it all!

Since, I've been at it for so goddamn long: problem-solving; decision-making;

designing; analyzing; evaluating; connecting; synthesizing; elaborating; imagining;

theorizing; strategizing; or, of my being a so-called story-teller; writer; typist; essayist;

poet; reader; editor; artist; designer; publisher; picture-taker; movie-maker; advertiser;

marketer; and, a shrewd student of long-lasting learning, and even more.

That, I just want and need to be on the damned go—or, *to just let go…!* Heave-ho...!

Ho-Ho-Ho!

The Blues

That's correct! On whatev'r day or night, it'll almost nev'r find her: mad-ness.

For such would be a great big NO-NO, or a great big NO-GO:

Her life being about—ev'n, a teeny-bit of Sad-ness.

That's right! It's good if not great to know.

That, indeed, her fantastically fine life only adds to her present-day glad-ness.

Moral Fiber

Why do they want or need to be a part of such nation?

Is it a super sensational station that dreams of being righted?

By chance, that's why the right nightmares are in-born, so in-arguably, or rightly, in the pretty penny-pinching, invitations?

To make damn sure—that, wobbly lives—still, will be more than just blighted?

Do I've to really relate such roundly relatable revelations?

That is, who amid us doesn't desire Honor—or, Character—or, even, a richly inherited spirit?

Whose status and stature both—in life, often, allows the absolutely apt Aces a great big benefit in life's giant race?

Whose damn'd base pace is all about the goddamn'd circular chase to just save face?

Loss of Face

It's something that the head-strong and hard-pressed man can't and won't stand for—
Dis-honor.

That it's been, almost, certainly, the norm, although others in life's snake-eat-dog, fight, have tried, so tirelessly, to deface his near noble cause or title.

Still, the man has tried, almost, always, to keep such folk way under his power. As it's no shame, for it's the only way—in which, to maintain such grip—much tighter! That's correct! Since, his aim is, almost, nev'r, to become, in any way, what so ev'r, a down-right downer; but, will remain, forev'r, a fabulously fit fighter of a causative founder.

Afterword

Is assorted poetry best?

In my opinion, I surely think so. This is to say, that it can be good if not great; to construct an assortment of fixed and un-fixed poems. The former—fixed is rhymed like a sonnet; and, the latter—un-fixed is un-rhymed like free-verse. Poetically, to be able to construct an assortment of poems, schematically, and, stylistically, and, even, randomly, without regard; to some set law(s), is truly, what poeticizing is all about. In other words, to be able to use one's "poetic license," so utilizing all conventionally/un-conventionally poetic devices; to effectuate a certain affect/effect; in conveying thoughts and feelings either loftily or impassionately and imaginatively—freely; all of which, makes for some attention-grabbing if not some distinctive poems.

Such is true, so particularly, in the case of constructing free-verse poetry or even prose-poetry. That does not conform, so automatically, to certain kinds of rhymes or the mixture thereof: masculine; feminine; slant; perfect; or rhyme schemes—aa, aba, abab, ababa, ababab…; poems—couplets—aa, bb, cc, dd, ee…; terza rimes—aba, bcb, cdc, ded, efe…; quatrains—abab, cdcd, efef, ghgh, ijij…; or even varied sonnets—typically, 14 lines of poetry as, in a Shakespearean sonnet—abab, cdcd, efef, gg; Petrarchan (Italian) sonnet—abbaabba, cdecde; Spenserian sonnet—abab, bcbc, cdcd, ee; none of which, yet again, conforms, so automatically, to free-verse poetry or even prose-poetry. Enduring such…, what about form and rhythm; both of which—rhythm, and form—are almost always seen in pre-set poems?

We have to question such question with another/other question/s: Why decline if not forfeit an address, a memory, or an observational, or even an allusive poem, and so on; just, to attain some pre-set form or rhythm, poetically? Why discount, or, better yet, disavow, and, so out-rightly, such poetic tools as provocation; imagism; automatism; or, automatic writing, and so forth; just, to obtain if not attain some pre-set rhythm or form, poetically? Right, at the end of the day, what is the exact exchange of not metering some poem; whose metrical lines may or may not give some poet some pretty poetic freedom, or lots of liberty, so poetically? I presume if not assume that such final question will be problematic, perpetually. Just, the same, why not treat your self to such an assortment of poetry, meantime?

www.ingramcontent.com/pod-product-compliance
Lightning Source LLC
Chambersburg PA
CBHW081229020426
42331CB00012B/3100